AFFIRMATIONS FROM THE HEART

Nakya A. Dozier

This book was started as the written record of my journey in life. It was created so that I could look back and see how far I had travelled through the course of a year in specific areas of my life. There originally were no subtitles or divisions. Just a girl writing her feelings but, along the way, it became something more. I started to see a definition to what I was writing. I saw themes of what my life boiled down to when it came to my relationship with God. There were 5 areas that over the course of a year and a half, were greatly impacted – Love, Trust, Belief/Faith, Patience, and Self-Proclamation/Empowerment.

I began this book in late 2016. It has been a labor or love, a struggle, a joy, and a bucket of tears that has ended with it being published in 2023. That's 7 years of me sitting on this blessing. I wasn't going to publish it at first, but God spoke. My issue was fear. I allowed the devil to stop me from pushing through to my next. I allowed him to sit on this spiritual shift. Then an awakening happened. My ears opened to what God was speaking, what He had been speaking all along. My goal has never been to sell 100,000 copies. This book in fact is proof to myself of what God said I can do.

This book is dedicated to God first for the covenant relationship between He and I. I thank You Oh, Lord for being my ***Everything***. I thank You for loving me so much that You pushed me out of my fear, out of my comfort zone and into Your light. I understand that obedience is better than sacrifice and trust that Your way is illuminated with grace, mercy, but most importantly, love.

Secondly, I must thank my parents Valarie and (the late) William "Bro" Dozier. You have been my backbone way before I needed one. Thank you for loving and guiding me along this journey. You have been there every step of the way.

To my son, Taron, and siblings – I love you and thank you for loving me enough to be the hands on my back and the extra push that I needed.

To my spiritual parents, Apostle Hope L. and Elder Erskine Daniels and Pastor Glen E. Jenkins and my spiritual big sisters, Pastor Sharise Harrison, Elder Gloria Jackson and Lia Henderson, you are always there, praying and covering me. I thank you for being living epistles, easily read by men (2 Corinthians 3:2-3).

To all my aunts, uncles, cousins, nieces, nephews, and godparents (Aunt Saundra, Uncle Frog, Aunt Barbara, and (the late) Uncle Jack – I Love you dearly. Thank you for loving me.

To my inner circle – Diehdre, Cheryl, Lia, Gloria, Rosie, Stacey – you are 6 rocks that don't mind straightening me out when I am so off course. I thank you for the guidance that comes from the heart.

I hope you all enjoy the Affirmations that God has given to me. They are a lot like my blog – Bro's Daughter. Find us at https://www.brosdaughter.com/. Thank you to those that already read along with me. The blog was my first step, and this book has become the second. We'll see where the Lord leads me next. ?

May God Bless and keep you. Thank you for your support and remember….

Be A Blessing and Not Just Blessed!!!

Love,
Nakya

Table of Contents

Love

Love

Love is that one emotion that all humans crave. It is that thing that makes your heart beat or feel as if it is breaking into. Love is by many definitions the "be all that end all". If you have someone that loves you, then life is perfect. But love can divide into many different categories. It isn't just romantic love that makes us happy. There is a parental love that makes us smile with delight when we see our offspring or are embraced by our parents. There is a friendship love that makes us want to spend time with our friends.

However, human love at its best is fickle and fleeting. In a world where not just celebrities but the working class are marrying today and divorcing tomorrow, you learn not to trust people and to guard your heart. You would think that guarding your heart would keep you from getting hurt, but it only helps you shut down the most powerful and sustaining emotion that a human being can experience.

The best love comes from the original source – the Lord thy God. His love is better than any we have ever experienced. It cradles us in His arms and offers forgiveness even before we can utter the words. His love has been with us since our beginning as Jeremiah 29:11 testifies. It is proof that He has always been with us, guiding and loving us through life. Being right there as the shoulder to cry on and the cheerleader when all goes right in our world. As our Father, He also scolds us when we are wrong to ensure that we don't continue to repeat the same mistake. But, even if we do, His love never fails or waivers. God's love lasts from everlasting to everlasting. Meaning that it was here before time began and will continue when time ends.

Here are a few examples of that love that have strengthened my heart and renewed my sense of well-being, allowing me the opportunity to open the door for others to fully come on in.

Love

SELF CONDEMNATION

"My dear children, let's not just talk about love; let's practice real love. This is the only way we'll know we're living truly, living in God's reality. It's also the way to shut down debilitating self-criticism, even when there is something to it. For God is greater than our worried hearts and knows more about us than we do ourselves." (I John 3:18-20, MSG)

It is easy to condemn ourselves because above all others, we know what we do. We are with ourselves every waking second of everyday. It is easy to fool others but fooling oneself takes a lot of work.

Yet, God commands us to love not just our neighbors but ourselves too. Living in love is a way of life. Real love doesn't taunt or condemn. It knows you have faults but sees the goodness inside of you. Real love – God's Love – is the only true cleansing mechanism that we can use to love ourselves. It is the healing balm to broken hearts, minds, and souls.

When you let God's love flow freely within, it will then flow freely on the exterior of you too.

Love

JUDGEMENT COMES

"There is one lawgiver, who is able to save and to destroy: who art thou that judgest another?" (James 4:12, KJV)

Judgement is something we all do. Ever been out somewhere and you see a woman in tight-tight clothes where nothing of her body is a mystery? What's your first thought? Did you judge her? God is the only one whom has a right to judge. He is the only one that can tell someone whether they are right or wrong. Don't get caught with stones in your hands lest God changes the person you cast them at into rubber. "I'm rubber, you're glue. Whatever you say bounces off me and sticks to you." A child-like chant that holds much water.

Yes, we are to be each other's keeper, however, we are to neither condemn or condone another's actions. I've heard it said that you can lead a horse to water, but you can't make them drink. Well, you can tell someone the truth, but you can't make them accept it. When we take it upon ourselves to force people to see the light, we have stepped into an area of judgment. We've left behind being our brother's keeper and tried to become their God. Be careful in this arena.

Judgest not. Condemn not. Love them and allow God to move. He is the Potter so allow Him to mold His clay the way He sees fit.

Love

LOVE IS PATIENT

"Love is patient, love is kind. It does not envy, it does not boast· it is not proud" (I Corinthians 13:4, NIV)

Oft we look to others to fill a void in our lives. We think that hearing the words "I Love You" truly means that that person loves you. While the love of a parent, child, sibling, spouse, or close friend is often true, there is not greater love than that of God. His love is patient when we mess up. His love fills all voids and heals all pain. God is our one true love. That love that gives you the warm fuzzies which never go away.

Our job is to wait for God. Yes, waiting is hard, but patience is a virtue that we all need to strive for. Patiently waiting doesn't mean that you give up. It does mean that you dig deeper into your Word and into your relationship with the Creator. Take the time during your waiting to find out what God wants of you.

Love springs eternal. Ever heard that? Imagine the well of God's love. I can see it being so deep in the earth that there is no ending nor beginning.

Love

THE JOY OF THE LORD

"[10] Then Ezra said to them, "Go [your way], eat the rich festival food, drink the sweet drink, and send portions to him for whom nothing is prepared; for this day is holy to our Lord. And do not be worried, for the joy of the LORD is your strength and your stronghold". (Nehemiah 8:10, AMP)

Some time ago, the words – The joy of the Lord is your strength – kept resonating in my spirit. I'd been hearing it for four months. I got so happy over that portion that I had to do a double take when I read the same scripture in the Amplified Bible *"...the joy of the Lord is your strength and your stronghold".* Wait, hold up. I thought strongholds were bad evil things that we needed to get rid of. But, if His joy is my strength and my stronghold then this is one stronghold that I must hold fast too.

Strongholds. I was taught were things that bounded you and kept you from God's light. Definition - to fortify through the idea of holding safely; a castle, fortress, fastness, anything on which one relies. So, His joy is what I should rely on? His joy is my castle – that place where I should live. His joy holds me safely. Hold up!! His joy – His joy – His joy. Getting it yet? This is the stronghold I want in my life. That which is pure and loving. That which cares for me like no other. That which edifies me and pushes me to righteousness.

Love

THANK GOD FOR THE BLOOD

"But the children of Israel committed a trespass in the accursed thing: for Achan, the son of Carmi, the son of Zabdi, the son of Zerah, of the tribe of Judah, took of the accursed thing: and the anger of the LORD *was kindled against the children of Israel." (Joshua 7:1, KJV)*

In reading Joshua 7, you see the "other side" of God, the vengeful side. Not the grace giving God that we have been taught. In this book, a man Achan, is murdered on God's decree for not following God's Word when they children of Israel took the city of Jericho.

After reading this, my first thought was – thank God for the blood that covers my sins. Thank God for Jesus Christ who was the sacrificial lamb without blemish who now sits on the right hand of the Father interceding daily for me. But what happens when grace is done? Judgement. Are you ready for it? Are any of us?

Thankfully, we are still in a season where God's love and grace reign. What a perfect time to rededicate ourselves to the Master and Ruler of everything. We call on the blood but are we applying it? Are we putting it on the doorposts of our hearts, mind, ears, eyes? We can thank Him for the blood all day, but its power came when the children of Israel applied it to the doorposts.

Love

CAN WE ALL GET ALONG?

"I appeal to you, brothers and sisters, in the name of our Lord Jesus Christ, that all of you agree with one another in what you say and that there be no divisions among you, but that you be perfectly united in mind and thought." (I Corinthians 1:10, NIV)

Paul is speaking to the church of Corinth. He is speaking directly to Christians regarding the way they have been getting along. What is it about Christians that we get into church, become saved, start working on behalf of the gospel and then fall apart. We get into clicks, divide into groups. Paul points out our own weaknesses – "I don't see many of the brightest and the best among you, not many influential, not many from high-society families. Isn't it obvious that God deliberately chose men and women that the culture overlooks and exploits and abuses, chose these 'nobodies' to expose the hollow pretenses of the somebodies" (I Corinthians 1:26-31, MSG).

Why then do we get high and mighty when we get into church? Why do we get to a point that we think its our church. No! The church, the building, the chairs/pews, the instruments, bathrooms, hallways, people, and everything else belong to God. We are His instruments. He is not ours. Let us take this message and hear God's warning in it. Let us stop thinking more highly of ourselves than we are to the point that we believe that its okay to dictate to others who and/or what they are, not to mention their self-worth. God picked the least among them. Where do you fall in society? Better yet, where do you think you fall?

Patience

Patience

I've heard many times in my life that Patience is a virtue. As a child, I had no idea what virtue was, but I understood that it was something that I needed to have. As I got older, I understood virtue to mean, that patience was a moral standard that everyone should aspire to. It is something that we should all strive to obtain and keep for all our lives. Patience then became this tangible item that I began striving to obtain. However, it seemed the more I tried to be patient, the more my patience was tested. Come ON!!! It seemed the closer I got to a goal, someone would move the finish line and the farther the goal became from where I was. Imagine running a marathon. You've been running for 2 hours and can now see the finish line. Then suddenly, the 2 people holding the rope at the end move 10 feet away in the opposite direction. Yep!! This is what it felt like as a single parent trying to save money to get ahead. As an employee trying to climb the ladder of success. As a human, trying to be righteous and upright. Someone was continually moving that dang goal line.

The best discovery that I've had in this walk is that I needed to stop judging myself by the standards of others. I needed not to judge my life by the humanly goals I achieved but by God's pleasure in my life. If God is pleased, then does it truly matter if the house wife down the street was angry that I sent in store brought and not homemade cupcakes for the class Christmas party? Did it matter that my boss who has no kids was angry that I had to take a sick day when my son had a temperature over 100 degrees?

Learning to accept my current state of being caused me to be patient with myself. These next few pages helped the journey along the way.

Patience

THE PROMISE IS WORTH WAITING FOR

"On one occasion, while he was eating with them, he gave them this command: "Do not leave Jerusalem, but wait for the gift my Father promised, which you have heard me speak about." (Acts 1:4, NIV)

"[5]I wait for the LORD, my whole being waits, and in his word, I put my hope. [6]I wait for the Lord more than watchmen wait for the morning, more than watchmen wait for the morning." (Psalm 130:5-6, NIV)

"Since ancient times no one has heard, no ear has perceived, no eye has seen any God besides you, who acts on behalf of those who wait for him." (Isaiah 64:4, NIV)

As a single woman, I wait on the time that I will be called wife. Yet, in my waiting season, I don't sit idly by. It is my job to strengthen my walk with God. It is hard to walk blindly in this thing called "faith". Yet, walk blindly I must. I must trust and believe in this promise.

I watched this Facebook video where God told this man of the daughter he would have. The man was 12 during this conversation with God. It was many years later when this promise was fulfilled. The man had been married four and a half years before the promise was seen when God blessed him with the child of his heart – an adopted newborn daughter that God named Chloe.

God's promises are always fulfilled. We must wait until it is time for us to see the physical manifestation. Promises from God don't go unanswered, nor do they drop to the ground and wither away. These promises will come to pass as did the earth on the verbal command of the Lord thy God.

Patience

AMUSEMENT OR PURPOSE

"11To bring Vashti the queen before the king with the crown royal, to shew the people and the princes her beauty: for she was fair to look on.12 But the queen Vashti refused to come at the king's commandment by his chamberlains: therefore was the king very wroth, and his anger burned in him." (Esther 1:11-12, KJV)

During a drunken state, King Ahasuerus sent for Queen Vashti, to show her off in front of his friends. She refused. To defy the king??? How dare she!!! Queen Vashti wasn't beheaded. She was packed up and moved out of the king's house to never come before him again.

Yet, had she not, she wouldn't have been cast out and Esther wouldn't have been crowned queen in her place. By becoming Queen, Esther was positioned in a place to save her people from death as ordered by a mad man.

Your purpose will move on your behalf. It will move people out of the positions that God has ordained for you at your appointed season. All you have to do is wait for the season.

Patience

HE'LL DO IT AGAIN

"[1]Early in the morning Joshua and all the Israelites set out from Shittim and went to the Jordan, where they camped before crossing over. [11] See, the ark of the covenant of the Lord of all the earth will go into the Jordan ahead of you. [12] Now then, choose twelve men from the tribes of Israel, one from each tribe. [13] And as soon as the priests who carry the ark of the LORD—the Lord of all the earth set foot in the Jordan, its waters flowing downstream will be cut off and stand up in a heap." (Joshua 3:1,11-13, NIV)

Some years ago, there was a very popular song by a Christian singer that spoke of God's ability to do today what He had done before. The chorus goes on to tell us that He's the same God yesterday, today, and tomorrow. It amazes me when I read the Bible how many times God shows this sentiment.

Most of us know adamantly of His parting of the Red Sea when the Israelites left Egypt after the 10 plagues. But how many know the story of the parting of the Jordan River after God's appointment of Joshua to lead the Israelites to the promised land? Here, God parted the Jordan and had the Ark of the Covenant carried by the priest into the water, they stopped mid-way, and the people came through. Then, God did something He hadn't done at the Red Sea. He instructed Joshua to select twelve men, one from each family, to get 1 stone from the middle of the Jordan where the priests feet stood and to build a memorial (alter).

The parting of the sea wasn't new. The people grew up hearing the testimonies of their ancestors of how God had parted the sea. He'd done it before – provided a way out of no way. He'd done it once to get them away from their enemies and a second time to make a path to conquer the land He had promised them. God provided a way for His people each time a need arose wherein they couldn't see it.

Hasn't He done the same for us? Provided a way out when you didn't see one. Whether before or after your acknowledgement of your salvation. God was there forging a path. If He did it before.......

Patience

MEDITATE

"Keep this Book of the Law always on your lips; meditate on it day and night, so that you may be careful to do everything written in it. Then you will be prosperous and successful." (Joshua 1:8)

Meditate – focusing on something in a calm and relaxed environment. I once taught youth Sunday school where we did an exercise on meditating. It was hard for the kids – especially the younger ones who had no idea of how to be calm.

But this lesson would have been just as hard for some adults. Life happens and distractions come. How tempting would it be to answer a kid yelling "Ma" at the top of their lungs even when you know nothing is wrong. Meditation takes focus. So does staying in God's will. Meditate on His Word day and night. Hide it in your heart and store it in your soul so that when life happens, you'll have guidance as to what to do.

Here's an easy introduction. Sit in a quiet place after your house has settled for the night. Sit and be still. Listen and wait. God is speaking. Are you hearing?

Patience

WHERE IS YOUR JOY?

"[14] And David danced before the LORD with all his might, wearing a priestly garment. [15] So David and all the people of Israel brought up the Ark of the LORD with shouts of joy and the blowing of rams' horns." (II Samuel 6:14-15, NIV)

Sitting in traffic can be horrible. While living in the DC Metro area, I hated driving outside of my local area and forget driving to or through DC. One day, however, I decided to make it a fun adventure instead of a chore. I put on some of my favorite music and danced the whole hour it took me to travel the les than ten miles to work.

Trials come and go but God's joy is always available to us. How do you spend your time during a trial? Mad? Frustrated? Angry? I decided while sitting in traffic that if I had to have a party all by myself, then that's what I would do. Did the traffic change? Nope. But my outlook did. I got through the traffic and yes, I was late to work. However, it was my attitude that made the difference in the rest of my day.

People looked at me and shook their heads. Maybe some thought, I was crazy. Maybe others couldn't comprehend why this silly woman was dancing while the traffic was slowly, slowly creeping by. But none of that mattered to me. None of their opinions on my situation could alter my opinion of how I was going to endure this trial. At one point, I witnessed another person dancing right along with me, so I began to rejoice that someone else had joined the party. I saw another person not allowing their circumstances to dictate their attitude.

My patience could have been worn thin by the time I got to my desk. But a change in perspective changed the flow and rhythm of the remainder of my day. Next time you are in traffic or faced with a stressful situation, host and attend your own party!

Patience

WAITING

"[2] Consider it pure joy, my brothers and sisters, whenever you face trials of many kinds, [3] because you know that the testing of your faith produces perseverance." (James 1:2-3, NIV)

I have this magnet that was given to me with a quote that tells the reader to be confident in the path before us as we travel the road of dreams and to live the life that our imagination produces. Little did the person who gave this to me know that I was planning to uproot my life and relocate out of state.

What I've learned over the years is that living the life I've imagined takes time. Patience. What many of us have little of but what all of us need. Not everything we desire comes over night or with the snap of a finger. Many times, that which we desire is more than worth the wait.

Think of that one thing that you want. Could you truly handle it now at this stage in your life? Are you truly ready for that blessing? Sometimes God holds onto the blessing until we have truly prepared ourselves not only to receive it but when we know how to handle/manage it. While you wait for the blessing, prepare yourself for it. Let's say you are waiting for your business to take off, how are you preparing for that? What protocol have you set in place?

Patience is the waiting place for the blessing. Be ye ready for the season when it comes to you.

Trust

Trust

Trust can be used as a noun or verb. As a noun, it means that you rely on a person or thing, that you have confidence or confidently expect something, that you have hope. I can trust that a water slide at an amusement park will hold my weight because I trust that it has been tried. Trust can also be a verb in you showing your confidence in someone or something. I remember the first event I ever published (for lack of a better term) by myself. It was a success. I grew confidence in my abilities to do the work. I trusted that what I had been taught would earn me success in my field.

Trust in its most basic form when used as a verb is when we put our walls down and allow people in. I can trust that you will be a good friend because you've proven to be so thus far. We all have levels of trust. I may trust my brother to go into my home while I'm away on travel, but I don't trust my neighbor to do the same. Some feel that trust is earned while others give it freely.

For many humans - trust is that thing that if broken can be hard to get back, if ever given back. Aren't we glad that God doesn't use the same trust meter that we do? How many times have we leaned onto our own understanding, trusting that we had the right information to gage a situation only to learn that we were missing key factors. Trust. God trusts us. But do we trust Him? So many times, God has only given me glimpses into a situation. I had to trust Him and rely on His direction. Trusting God is part of our foundational relationship with Him. If we trust Him as we say we do, this journey could be so easy.

Along the way, my trust in God has grown. Here are a few of the lessons I've learned along the way.

Trust

BATTLE OF WILLS

"Submit yourselves therefore to God. Resist the devil, and he will flee from you." (James 4:7, KJV)

Submission has become an ugly word. People believe that being submissive means that you have no opinion and allow others to walk all over you. That's not submission. I can submit to God and not be the doormat for mankind.

Surrendering to God means releasing control of your life, body, and mind to Him. So, let's think about this. By releasing control or surrendering, I'm letting go of all my stresses and stressors – finances, significant others, children, job, gossip, car troubles, and on and on. I'm giving God all my problems and being left with what – joy, happiness, peace, love? Why not submit? Possibly because I am a control freak and can't imagine anyone else, not even God, juggling all these areas of my life. But I've got to decide, because my mess has become too much weight for me to bear. Do I release control and trust that God can handle it all or do I continue the patch that I've been on continuing to juggle all and praying that this mess doesn't fall down on top of my head?

Which would you choose?

Trust

GOD'S MANAGEMENT OF YOUR LIFE

"For I the LORD thy God will hold thy right hand, saying unto thee, Fear not; I will help thee." (Isaiah 41:13, KJV)

We get so set on how our life should be, how we should do this or that. Yet, we forget that God is the manager of our lives. He neither needs nor wants us to walk through this life without Him. As our Lord, our controller, our comptroller, He has a plan/design for our lives. All we must do is extend our hand so that He can take control.

In asking for help, we must let the helper do the job. June of 2016, my mom came up to the house to help get my son ready for his high school graduation. I had this task that was daunting for me and asked her to take control of it. Yet, when she began to clear things out, I felt as if I was losing control. Crazy!! Here, I was the one asking for the help, yet I didn't' receive it. She said to me, "How can someone ask for help yet stop the person helping?" Mom's and their wisdom, right? I was immediately contrite because I stood in the way of the of the task getting completed. I was the fool that stood in the road yelling – NO!!!! – when my control had been taken away.

This encounter is not different than what we do with God. We go to Him begging, pleading, crying for help, grace, and mercy. When He steps in and clears out our junk, we cry "No, stop" because it never feels good to let go of that which we had been holding onto forever. But, as with the case with my mom, the clearing is for the best. That thing which I'm struggling with, He has ultimate control to manage or remove it.

Let God have total control. I'll guarantee that He'll replace the thing He removes with something 100 times better.

Trust

COMPLETE UNDERSTANDING

"1" What causes fights and quarrels among you? Don't they come from your desires that battle within you? 2 You desire but do not have, so you kill. You covet but you cannot get what you want, so you quarrel and fight. You do not have because you do not ask God.3 When you ask, you do not receive, because you ask with wrong motives, that you may spend what you get on your pleasures. 4 You adulterous people, don't you know that friendship with the world means enmity against God? Therefore, anyone who chooses to be a friend of the world becomes an enemy of God. 5 Or do you think Scripture says without reason that he jealously longs for the spirit he has caused to dwell in us? 6 But he gives us more grace. That is why Scripture says: "God opposes the proud but shows favor to the humble." Submit yourselves, then, to God. Resist the devil, and he will flee from you. 8 Come near to God and he will come near to you. Wash your hands, you sinners, and purify your hearts, you double-minded. 9 Grieve, mourn and wail. Change your laughter to mourning and your joy to gloom." (James 4:1-9, NIV)

I was reading the other day and came across an email with James 4:9: Your laughter must change to mourning and your joy to sorrow". This threw me. So you're telling me to no longer have this feeling of inner peace – this euphoric feeling that all will be, okay? This sent me in a whirlwind. Being me, I had to look up the scripture. I needed a complete understanding of the Word and in what application it was being used.

James 4:1 discusses those that aren't living a Godly life. Those fighting and quarrelling. Those that are living in and of the world. Those that want the blessings that they can see and feel. But James 4:7 is where the direction begins to turn – submit yourselves…hand over your control. Get away from that which means you no good, "Wash your hands, you sinners, and purify your hearts, you double-minded (James 4:8) then James 4:9 your laughter must change to mourning and your joy to sorrow.

Your laughter and joy before your submission were worldly – fleshly. They were brought out when your flesh felt good. Changing your worldly laughter and joy means that you are no longer entertaining things that mean you no good – drugs, people, attitudes, desires of grandeur.

So, yes – change your laughter and your joy!!! But know why you need to change them. As with any scripture, ensure you know the content and context of God's meaning. Scripture out of context is dangerous and can lead you to your fall. Just ask Eve who listened to the snake as he used scripture out of context.

Trust

THE WILL IN THE MIDDLE OF THE WILL

"16 This was the appearance and structure of the wheels: They sparkled like topaz, and all four looked alike. Each appeared to be made like a wheel intersecting a wheel." (Ezekiel 1:16, NIV)

Our will often contradicts God's will. We wonder why we struggle. Why we have it so hard when others seem to be floating by. Truth is – no one is floating. We all have our own struggles. Years ago, before I recognized The Savior as My Savior, I heard this song – more money, more problems. I laughed and said, well send me more money and I'll see if I have more problems.

Sitting in church one day, there was a speaker who prayed over me. Her prayer while simple was powerful. She prayed that I would allow God's will to take hold of my life and that I would stay on the wheel so that The Potter could mold me. Problem then, as it has been all of my life- I'm stubborn and like to have things my way. My way though has earned me a rough road in dry land.

So, I pray today what she prayed that day (note that this is my personal prayer and not her words) .... "Father, humbling myself unto Thy throne, I give you all control over all things involving me. I release all unto You God. Allow me to stay within Your will. Allow me to follow Your will even when I don't see it. Let me stay on bended knee at Your voice and acknowledge Your presence within every aspect of my life allowing You to be the wheel and me the vessel so that I can walk upright in Your sight."

Trust

TESTED + TRIED = TRUST

"[1] In you, LORD my God, I put my trust. [2] I trust in you; do not let me be put to shame, nor let my enemies' triumph over me.[3] No one who hopes in you will ever be put to shame, but shame will come on those who are treacherous without cause. [4] Show me your ways, LORD, teach me your paths. [5] Guide me in your truth and teach me, for you are God my Savior, and my hope is in you all day long." (Psalm 25: 1-5, NIV).

Trust. It is not a word easily used nor a word easily given. For many, trust is the right of passage within a friendship – or any relationship. In terms of human nature, trust comes after you have been tested and tried then found true.

Trust. In the heavenly realm, comes when you learn that God will neve leave you, that He carries us through the trials. How? How do we learn to trust Him? Reading (His Word). Studying (His Word). Communication (praying to Him then listening for His answer).

Gideon was a soldier, one used to taking orders. Yet, he questioned God's command to go to Midian and wage war. So, he tested God with a simple little piece of fleece. Judges 6:36 reads "If thou wilt save Israel by mine hand as thou hast said….". Small words but meaningful. God knows His children. He knows which of us will go with blind faith and which will ask questions. He tells us to ask, seek, knock 9(Matthew 7:7). He's already prepared to answer any questions you have. We must be ready for His answer. Then as Gideon did, trust that He knows what He is doing and who He is sending into battle. The test of trust is not in the action of the test. It is in the action of submission unto His will.

Trust

RUSHING PAST THE MIRACLE

"28 "Lord, if it's you," Peter replied, "tell me to come to you on the water."29 "Come," he said. Then Peter got down out of the boat, walked on the water and came toward Jesus." (Matthew 14:28-29)

This is a famous passage of scripture. Almost every believer knows it. It's the passage where the disciples are in the boat and the winds are blowing. They get scared as the boat is tossed to and fro, they see Jesus walking toward them on the water. Peter asks to come to Him.

At a conference some years ago, I was reminded of this scripture. I was reminded of this miracle. Yes, Peter ends up falling because He takes his eyes off Jesus. For most sermons regarding this passage of scripture, his falling is the focus. But let's forget that for a moment. Let's look at the miracle – Peter walked on water!!! Jesus said come. Peter trusted. Peter did as Jesus instructed and look at the miracle.

We don't always get it right. But we should rejoice in the times when we trust Jesus and He makes a miracle happen. We cannot continue to rush past the things that Jesus is doing because it doesn't look like, feel like or seem like its right. We cannot ignore the fact that we are stronger today than we were yesterday or that we are growing closer to God each and every day. When we rush past the miracle, its saying that the miracle was insignificant. Rejoice even in the little things. How can God give you something big to celebrate when you haven't enjoyed the journey and the conquering along the way? Each small victory is a chance to celebrate the miracle. So……it's time to celebrate.

Belief/Faith

Belief/Faith

My belief says I can even when my eyes don't see. My faith says I will even when my belief rocks. It took months, years of faith in God to write this book. I had a dream the week that I went to publish. On my left side was my spiritual mother, Apostle Hope L. Daniels and on my right was my natural mother, Valarie A. Dozier. Both urged me to write the book. I understood God to say that here is where my natural talent had to meet my spiritual gifts. I had to take what I knew I could do and allow God to use them the way He sees fit. I sat the night before I pushed myself to finish this book and read stories, books that I have started and never finished. There are so many of them. What I realized was that I do have talent. So, what was holding me up? Doubt in myself. Doubt that anyone would read the book, buy the book. That the book would be waste of space. But mostly, that others wouldn't see me in each line. Wouldn't get the message.

Here's the problem with doubt, it's all about you. Faith is the opposite. Faith moves based on God's say. If I believe that God made the heavens and the earth. If I believe that He knows my beginning and end, then I should have no doubt that when He says to do something, He has a plan for what's to come. Move by His Word as you sit in His will and let God be God. He got this!! Move you out of the way and live according to His way. His ways are truly higher than ours.

And, onto the next area of my life where God had to show me, me.

Belief/Faith

WHICH COMETH YOUR HELP

"I will lift up mine eyes unto the hills, from whence cometh my help. My help cometh from the Lord, which made heaven and earth." (Psalm 121:1-2, KJV)

People often say look to Jesus because He is your help. But what does it really mean? It means just what it says. Jesus is your help in all matters big and small. Once if you've established a relationship with Jesus, you realize the power that He has. Power that He endows you with to face everyday obstacles and challenges.

Human relationships take time. Years ago, I told a man I was dating that I needed his time for our relationship to work. The relationship eventually ended because one party didn't want to put the time into it. I realized later that God was saying the same thing to me.

If you've been living a life where you relied only on yourself, it will take time, trials, and tribulations for you to build your trust in God. God gives us these trials and tribulations daily. So what, when you first join a church, you rock your club skirt to the church? Been there, done that and He still chose me. Daily, God strengthens His relationship with us. But we have to be open to receive that which He has for us. Tribulations – your issues – don't come to break you. They come to show you that you are stronger than you think and that the Creator is always in your corner fighting for you. You may think, then why did I go thru this or that? Hurts and pain aren't there to condemn you. They can show you that the battle that you are trying to overcome really isn't your battle to overcome. Lift your head and look to the heavens, then focus on what you are looking at. Don't focus on the thing, person, situation that is causing the hurt. Focus on the one that is there to show you His power and strength that can overcome any challenge.

Belief/Faith

DOING YOUR PART

"7 "Now, LORD my God, you have made your servant king in place of my father David. But I am only a little child and do not know how to carry out my duties. 8 Your servant is here among the people you have chosen, a great people, too numerous to count or number. 9 So give your servant a discerning heart to govern your people and to distinguish between right and wrong. For who is able to govern this great people of yours?" 10 The Lord was pleased that Solomon had asked for this. 11 So God said to him, "Since you have asked for this and not for long life or wealth for yourself, nor have asked for the death of your enemies but for discernment in administering justice, 12 I will do what you have asked. I will give you a wise and discerning heart, so that there will never have anyone like you, nor will there ever be." (I Kings 3:7-12, NIV)

This passage tells the story of how King Solomon became to be so wise. He went to Gibeon to offer burnt offerings unto the Lord. At night, during his peaceful state, God came to Solomon and asked what he wanted. Solomon's answer was wisdom. Not riches, not destruction of his enemies, not territory. He wanted wisdom to govern God's people. Magnificent. The answer so pleased God that He gave him wisdom and more – riches and honor. But Solomon had to do his part in receiving God's gifts – walk in God's ways, keep His statues, and His commandments.

Blessings aren't earned by just asking for them. God gives unto us, but we have to do our part. 1. Ask for what is really needed. Solomon needed wisdom to rule God's people. 2. After receiving the blessing and the run-over, you still have to walk with God and remain holy as He is holy. Holiness is not a state of mind or a way of speaking. Holiness is a state of being, a way of life. Keeping God's commandments and statues. Keeping in close communication with God. Loving Him as He always loves you – without restrictions. Giving your all to God means giving all your mind, all your strength, all you heart.

Belief/Faith

IMPOSSIBLE......NOT!

"Cast all your anxiety on him because he cares for you." (I Peter 5:7)

We sometimes get so bogged down with life's miseries that we forget that we aren't supposed to carry tis weight. Daniel was thrown into the lion's den. David was chased by Saul. Abram had to take his beloved son to the mountain to sacrifice him. The widow fed the prophet her last. Ruth left her homeland to follow her mother-in-law. All these people were mighty examples of life's tragedies. Yet, each person preserved. Neither of them was alone. All had faith to see them thru their trials.

Where is your faith? Do you even believe that He cares for you? You can only cast your cares when you trust that the receiver can handle them. He is the Great, I Am. He can handle all things. He created all things didn't He!!! So, why can't he handle your junk?

Belief/Faith

WHICH WAY TO LEAN

"5 Trust in the LORD with all your heart and lean not on your own understanding;
6 in all your ways submit to him, and he will make your paths straight." (Proverbs 3:5-6, NIV)

In 2017, I purchased a 2018 calendar that was absolutely beautiful. The pictures were awesome but what took the calendar over the top were the inspiring words on each page. The cover stated how happiness came into our lives through doors we didn't leave open. How beautiful a sentiment. There have been many times that I received a euphoric feeling of happiness that came unexpectantly. I understand that the unexpected happened because my eyes were focused on God and doing His works. I wasn't thinking on what would bring me happiness but on what would make Him happy.

I remember asking Him before I did a specific task if it was something He wanted me to do. His confirmation came in a dream and when I performed the action, this overwhelming sense of happiness engulfed me. Lead your life not on what makes you happy but on what makes Him happy.

Belief/Faith

PRAYER OF JABEZ

"10 Jabez cried out to the God of Israel, "Oh, that you would bless me and enlarge my territory! Let your hand be with me and keep me from harm so that I will be free from pain." And God granted his request." (I Chronicles 4:10, NIV)

I've always wondered about this prayer. Why? Where did it come from? It wasn't until I took time to find it in the scriptures and research it that I realized that Jabez's family was part of the tribe of Judah.

Judah means praise. So, what if we expanded our praise? I've been taught that our praise is our tool – our weapon – to get us into the presence of God and the Word is what God uses to break down walls and destroy yokes. Using this equation, if I increase my praise, expand it, will more yokes be destroyed? I tried this and found that yes, when I expanded my praise, more yokes began to break off me. Repeatedly, the feelings that had me bound would loosen and then break or break off automatically.

Enlarge your praise so that you can taste and see that the Lord is good. When you do this, He can enlarge your territory so that you can get a better understanding of the God you serve.

Belief/Faith

OH LORD, WE PRAISE YOU

"When Jesus spoke again to the people, he said, "I am the light of the world. Whoever follows me will never walk in darkness but will have the light of life." (John 8:12, NIV)

People think praise is just saying Hallelujah or participating in song. Praise is part of your mindset. There is a song that says that even when going through a trial, praise is part of what they do. Storms bring trials and tribulation. Praise brings joy during the storms. Got issues? Then you should likewise have some praise. Instead of falling into worry and anxiety, which could open the door to depression, fall into praise.

God is light – THE LIGHT – and that's what He brings on the scene when you praise Him. He illuminates the path so you can find your way through.

Self-Proclamation/ Empowerment

Self-Proclamation/Empowerment

I used to belief that proclaiming myself as special was wrong. I thought by doing so that I was putting myself above others. It's been a battle in the last 10 years – yes, 10 years – to understand that loving myself isn't wrong nor self-elevation. It is self-empowerment. God believes that all His children are special. We are special quite simply because He made us that way. We each have something to offer this world that no one else has.

Growing up in a community where everyone knew my parents, siblings, cousins, aunts, and uncles, I was always 'the daughter of' or 'the sister of' or 'the niece of' or 'the cousin of' I didn't become "Nakya" until I went away to college in another city one and a half hours away. This is where I truly started exerting myself. However, without parents there to guide me, it was done in the wrong way. I went away from the lessons taught to me and the mantras spoken to me and walked a path that was all about me.

It wasn't until I recognized the salvation plan that God had already designed for me that I realized that this life truly isn't about me. While I am empowered, I am so to do His work and serve His people. This God given power isn't for riches and glory. It's for me to use so that others can see the light of God that lives in me and shines through me. This power is given so that I can be a living epistle, easily read by man – DAILY!!!

Proclaiming yourself special isn't evil if done in the right way – God's way. I AM SPECIAL unto the heavens. I am special because I was especially created for the God that I serve to be a servant unto His children. Here's what I've learned about cultivating my specialness correctly.

Self-Proclamation/Empowerment

I'M A SOLDIER

"No man that warreth entangleth himself with the affairs of this life; that he may please him who hath chosen him to be a soldier" (II Timothy 2:4, KJV)

There's this old song about being a soldier of the Lord – in His army. Soldiers are always on duty even when on vacation. Soldiers are trained in and out of classrooms. They study the enemy and their tactics. They exercise their minds and bodies to prepare for battles. Even if never called to fight, they are always ready.

Spiritual soldiers, however, must not only prepare their minds and bodies, but we must prepare our hearts and spirits as well. The best way to defeat the enemy is to use the weapon God has already given us. Our weapon is our sword. Our sword is the Word of God.

Stepping away from your duties at the church for a moment of time doesn't halt your duties as a solider. If anything, this is when your weapon should be used the most. Anyone can be a good solider when they line up with other soldiers. But what happens when you are away from your base of operations? Are you still using the Word of God? Do you slay the dragons with your tongue by speaking His love with His Word? Or do you slip back to being whom you were before and allow all the curse words to flow.

Real soldiers don't ever let their guard down. They stay alert at all times because the enemy is always walking to and fro trying to see whom he can devour.

Self-Proclamation/Empowerment

IGNORING THE MADNESS

"This they said, tempting him, that they might have to accuse him. But Jesus stooped down, and with his finger wrote on the ground, as though he heard them not." (John 8:6, KJV)

They brought her out. The adulterer. They brought her before Jesus. They wanted her stoned according to the law. They wanted to test Jesus. They tried to trap Him.

But Jesus bent down and started to write on the ground with His finger. He didn't immediately respond to their madness. It wasn't until they kept pushing that He gave then an answer – a perfect and just answer. *"He who is without [any] sin among you, let him be the first to throw a stone at her (AMP)."* And He went back to writing on the ground. The madness was ignored. The trappers were entangled in their own trap.

The woman didn't speak until the madness had been settled. She allowed Jesus to fight the battle waged against her. Ignoring the madness doesn't make you less than. It makes you smarter than. Having the last say, really isn't the last say. Jesus gets the final say. All we do is add to the fire of those trying to harm us. Why help them destroy you? Learning when to speak and when to be quiet is a key element when fighting a battle. After Jesus had His say, the crowd left as He wrote on the ground. When He looked back up, all the accusers were gone. He asked the woman who condemned her. Her only spoken word in these scriptures was that no one had condemned her. Jesus didn't condemn her either and sent her on her way.

Self-power isn't about speaking. Self-power is restraining oneself from fighting a battle that isn't yours to fight. It is your job to let Jesus fight your battles. It is your job to stand amid your accusers and let them do their job. Then wait and see the salvation of the Lord.

Self-Proclamation/Empowerment

TEMPTATION

"There hath no temptation taken you but such as is common to man: but God is faithful, who will not suffer you to be tempted above that ye are able; but will with the temptation also make a way to escape, that ye may be able to bear it." (I Corinthians 10:13, KJV)

Temptation can only tempt you if it appeals to you. If candy, money, a person, car, etc. is tempting to you, then it appeals to you. You can't blame others for what makes you weak in the knees. Want to stop giving into temptation, then start understanding why something or someone catches your eye. There is something in you that draws that person or thing to you. Find out what is inside you and stop blaming others. Prayer works!! Use it to help you overcome your temptations.

You know what also works? Fasting. Turn over the plate, turn off the television and social media, read the Word and soak in it. Yes, soak it up like a sponge so that you may withstand the fiery darts that are coming your way.

Self-Proclamation/Empowerment

LIVING IN PLENTY

"12 I know what it is to be in need, and I know what it is to have plenty. I have learned the secret of being content in any and every situation, whether well fed or hungry, whether living in plenty or in want. 13 I can do all this through him who gives me strength." (Philippians 4:12-13, NIV)

It has been said that we should know how to live in a variety of ways, whether with less or with plenty. Previously, I'd only lived in the land of less where you rob Peter to pay Paul (as the saying goes). During this time, I murmured and complained about the less all the time. See, I believed that I should have been farther along than I was. I was discouraged, empty, unhappy, and frustrated.

I've come to realize that I was living a less than life, not because it was what I deserved but because it was where I thought I deserved to be. Less than, not equal to, not worthy of. This is the land where I dwelled for years. The problem was that this place was never the place God designed for me.

God has promised a land of milk and honey. He promised an overflow. We must accept it and change our way of thinking. If you've never dreamed of more, then when the opportunity of more comes, you'll think it strange and yourself unworthy, uneducated, and even may even be intimidated by it. Don't be. Cast these thoughts into the pit of hell where they belong. You are so much more than these thoughts. May your talent and light spring forth eternal.

Self-Proclamation/Empowerment

OH TASTE AND SEE

"Taste and see that the LORD is good; blessed is the one who takes refuge in him." (Psalm 34:8, NIV)

A couple of years ago, there was a whipped crem commercial where they gave you the choice between the real stuff and the junk. Who would choose the junk? Crazy notion, but we do. We choose to believe junk about ourselves – I'm nothing, I can't do it, I'm not pretty enough, I'm not smart enough, I'm not…. Just junk!!!

God did not create junk. God created you!!! You are not junk. If you were, He would not have created you to be the way He wanted you to be. Your skin, hair, face, size, talents. All created by Him for you to get everything out of life that you deserve (according to His will of course.)

His Word says, oh taste and see that I am good. How can something good create something bad? If you take the time an see just how wonderful He is – how loving, He is – taste His goodness and see it in your life. All of us have been on the rollercoaster ride of life. Yet, you are still here. That's His goodness. If hell is ruling and reigning in your life, then ask yourself what lesson you are to learn from it. What is God trying to show you so that you can reach your destiny?

The King James Version of the remaining portion of the scripture says "…. blessed is the man that trust in Him" while the NIV reads "…blessed is the one who takes refuge in Him". Want to get out of your hell? Spend time with God so that you can taste His goodness. So, you can see His goodness manifest in your life.

Self-Proclamation/Empowerment

I AM MORE THAN YOU SEE

"Salmon the father of Boaz, whose mother was Rahab, Boaz the father of Obed, whose mother was Ruth, Obed the father of Jesse," (Matthew 1:5, NIV)

Her name was Rahab, but she wasn't just called by her name. She was also called by what her profession was – Rahab, the harlot. Yet, this harlot was God's chosen one in a land that was set for destruction. Her works and faith brought life to not only her but her family as well. You can tell a blessed soul by how they care about more than just themselves. When she asked to be sparred, she also asked for the lives of her family. And she was given it and much more.

The people of Jericho only saw her as the harlot. Yet here she is in the lineage of Jesus. This drives Jesus' statement – I will make you a fisher of men. Jesus never cared about the profession of His disciples. He cared about their hearts. He still does today. He cares not about what you do but about how you treat others. That doesn't mean that you get to do anything as when you know better, you do better. But, for those that don't know Jesus and the blessing of His love, their assignment is to just come to Him as they are – broken, confused, frustrated, ashamed.

Rahab was a fisherman on her job. She is credited with saving the lives of the spies. What will God allow people to credit you with? Are you walking in the newness of life daily? Are you pouring into others what God has poured into you? Give and it shall be given to you, pressed down, shaken together, shall men give unto your bosom. Many use this for financial purposes but it means so much more. Give love and it shall be given back. Give understanding and it will come back to you. What are you prepared to give?